Florence
Griffith Joyner

Florence *Griffith Joyner*

DAZZLING
OLYMPIAN

Nathan Aaseng

Lerner Publications Company ▪ Minneapolis

This book is available in two editions:
Library binding by Lerner Publications Company
Soft cover by First Avenue Editions
241 First Avenue North
Minneapolis, Minnesota 55401

LIBRARY OF CONGRESS CATALOGING-IN-PUBLICATION DATA

Aaseng, Nathan.
　　Florence Griffith Joyner: dazzling Olympian / Nathan
Aaseng.
　　　　p. cm. — (The Achievers)
　　Summary: A biography emphasizing the running career
of the Olympic gold medalist who set new records in the
1988 Games in Seoul.
　　ISBN 0-8225-0495-2 (lib. bdg.)
　　ISBN 0-8225-9587-7 (pbk.)
　　1. Griffith Joyner, Florence Delorez, 1959-　　—Juvenile
literature.　2. Runners (Sports)—United States—Biography
—Juvenile literature.　3. Sprinting—Juvenile literature.
4.　Olympics—Juvenile literature.　[1.　Griffith Joyner,
Florence Delorez, 1960-　　.　2. Runners (Sports)　3. Afro-
Americans—Biography.]　I. Title.　II. Series.
GV1061.15.G785A18　　1989
796.4'26—dc19
[B]
[92]　　　　　　　　　　　　　　　　　　　89-2278
　　　　　　　　　　　　　　　　　　　　CIP
　　　　　　　　　　　　　　　　　　　　AC

Manufactured in the United States of America

International Standard Book Number: 0-8225-0495-2 (lib. bdg.)
International Standard Book Number: 0-8225-9587-7 (pbk.)
Library of Congress Catalog Card Number: 89-2278

4　5　6　7　8　9　10　99　98　97　96　95　94　93　92　91

Contents

1
The Curtain Rises

The city of Indianapolis, Indiana, was broiling, as it had been the entire searing summer of 1988. The heat wave combined with the drama and tension to turn the stadium into a giant pressure cooker. This was the site of the United States Olympic Track and Field Trials. During the next two weeks, dreams would come true for the top three finishers in each event. They would win the honor of representing their country in the 1988 Olympics. For many others, though, dreams of a lifetime were about to be shattered. Years of sacrifice and effort would leave them a fraction of a second too slow or a few inches short.

Among the contestants were some of the most famous athletes in the history of track and field. Edwin Moses already owned two Olympic gold medals and had once gone more than 10 years without losing a 400-meter hurdles race. Mary Decker Slaney had been holder of the United States women's record at every distance from 800 meters to 10,000. Carl Lewis, winner of a record-tying four gold track and field medals in the previous Olympics, had set his sights on four more. Evelyn Ashford was back to defend her title as the world's fastest female. Jackie Joyner-Kersee was primed to show the world that she was, as many claimed, the greatest female athlete who ever lived.

Most spectators and reporters would be watching these long-reigning kings and queens of the sport.

Florence's appearance definitely gives her "star" appeal.

Only true track followers were aware of athletes such as Florence Griffith Joyner. Florence was expected to be in the thick of some of those heart-rending struggles for second and third place. If she did well, according to the experts, she could reclaim a spot on the Olympic team. And, if she was lucky, some reporter might even break away from superstar-gazing long enough to give her a brief mention in a news report.

Florence Griffith Joyner, however, did not follow the script when she came to Indianapolis. Instead of playing her supporting role, she jumped onto center stage, commanding the spotlight. Florence trotted to the starting line for her first race wearing a bright green bodysuit. One leg was covered right down to her shoes, one leg was bare. Her thick, dark hair flowed behind her, and long, colorful fingernails decorated her hands. Her bright, glistening appearance seemed a reflection of Florence's confidence. She had concentrated so much on her training that she felt she could show the crowd she was someone to watch.

By stealing the lead role from the well-known athletes, Florence was setting herself up for a devastating fall. Seasoned athletes do not think much of competitors who call attention to themselves without having the skill to back it up. Fellow sprinter Gwen Torrence summed up what many onlookers were thinking. "If you're going to wear outfits like that, then you'd better do something in them!"

2
First Steps

Florence Griffith Joyner was not the first of her family to put herself through a brutal test of will. Her mother, also named Florence, had twice steeled herself to take on hopeless odds in her search for success.

The first time came when the elder Florence was 20. Leaving a young son behind with her parents in North Carolina, she moved to California. It was her dream to become a model. The odds, however, were stacked too heavily against this country girl. She ended up sewing clothes for a living, and marrying Robert Griffith, an airline electronics engineer.

Her second bold move came in 1964, when the Griffiths were living in the Mojave Desert. Seeing no hope that the family's future would improve, she packed up her 11 children and left Robert. The place she found for restarting her dreams was a four-bedroom housing project in Watts, a poor section of Los Angeles. In a neighborhood that would be scarred by some of the worst riots in United States history, she set out to raise a large family by herself.

The seventh of her children was Florence Delorez, who had been born December 21, 1959. Dee Dee, as she was called, often noticed that her mother had a faraway look in her eyes. When she asked her mother what she was thinking about, the answer would come, "I just want to get you guys out of here. This is not home."

Florence's mother never gave up on that dream, despite the depressing surroundings. Florence later remarked about her childhood that, "we didn't know how poor we were. We were rich as a family." If her mother had to give up meals so her children could eat, she would. If she had to set strict rules to keep her children out of trouble, that was what she would do. Mrs. Griffith's children knew that when she said something, she meant business, and they rarely challenged her. Like her brothers and sisters, Dee Dee was not allowed to watch television on weekdays, and she had to be in bed with the lights out at 10 o'clock, even when she was in high school.

At the same time, Dee Dee found ways to express her stubborn independence. Although she was cheerful and popular, Dee Dee could go for days without speaking to anyone. She learned to enjoy books, especially poetry. She set goals for herself by faithfully keeping a diary, in which she demonstrated an already iron-willed resolve. She knew what she liked, and she was headstrong enough to do what she wanted without caring what anyone else thought of her.

As early as kindergarten, she had her own ideas of style. Dee Dee liked to arrange her hair so that one braid always stuck straight up. Kids at school would make fun of her. Instead of being hurt, she would just laugh with them. Gradually, her friends grew to appreciate her artistic talent with hair. Using skills learned from her grandmother, a beautician, Dee Dee styled hair for many of the girls in the neighborhood.

Later, in high school, Dee Dee decided she wanted a pet. Instead of getting a "normal" pet such as a dog or a cat, Dee Dee took home a boa constrictor. Few snakes have been treated as royally as this one was. Dee Dee enjoyed bathing it and rubbing it with lotion. Instead of being disgusted by the skin that the snake shed, she saved it and painted it in bright colors. She also liked to carry her pet around her neck, even outside the house. Once she was asked to leave a shopping mall because the sight of her coiling snake was scaring away customers!

As if her creative independence did not make her stand out enough, Dee Dee also proved to be an exceptional athlete. Her mom noticed her talent long before Dee Dee ever entered any competition. Even when Dee Dee walked, she floated around so smoothly and lightly that she reminded her mother of a ballerina. On visits to her father in the desert, Dee Dee did some early sprint training without intending to. She enjoyed chasing jackrabbits, one of the fastest animals on earth. When the girl decided she liked running, Mrs. Griffith encouraged her, as she encouraged any of her children whenever they developed new interests.

At the age of seven, Dee Dee entered a Sugar Ray Robinson Youth Foundation competition in Los Angeles. A 20-year quest to be the fastest runner was about to begin as Dee Dee waited for the starter's signal. Since she was running against other children and not jackrabbits, Dee Dee was able to beat them all. Then her quiet nature took over and she was too shy to look Sugar Ray in the eye at the awards ceremonies.

At Jordan High School in Los Angeles, Dee Dee Griffith set school records in the sprints and the long jump. Her efforts were overshadowed, however, by one of her competitors. Despite her best attempts, Griffith could not defeat another local girl named Valerie Brisco.

Both Florence and Brisco grew up in Watts and are less than a year apart in age. And like Florence, Valerie came from a large family. Valerie was encouraged to run by her older brother Robert, who was a high-school hurdler. When she was 14, Robert

Florence Griffen

In her senior photo from the Jordan High School year-book, Dee Dee's last name was misspelled.

was killed by a stray bullet while practicing on the track. Because the high school named its track after Robert, the students thought that everyone with the name Brisco must be able to run fast. Valerie decided to prove them right and joined the track team. She later dedicated her track career to Robert.

In her senior year in high school, Valerie was recruited by a young assistant track coach from California State University at Northridge (Cal State) named Bobby Kersee. There she would become team-mates with Florence Griffith.

3
Developing Her Talents

After graduating in 1978, Griffith decided to attend Cal State. The study habits encouraged by her mother had become a permanent part of her. She earned good grades while beginning work toward a business degree. At the same time, she did well running the 200-meter and 400-meter distances for the track team.

Griffith could not, however, overcome the problem that had always plagued her mother—lack of money. She had to drop out after her freshman year to earn the money to continue her education. But Cal State's sprint coach, Bobby Kersee, was not about to let this budding sprinter go without a fight. Kersee guided Griffith through a maze of forms and procedures so that she could receive financial aid.

Kersee proved to be an exceptional track coach.

His skills were in demand and, soon after he had brought Griffith back to Northridge, he moved on to a different job. In 1980, Kersee was lured to the University of California at Los Angeles (UCLA), one of the track powers of college athletics. Griffith, encouraged by the excitement of high-speed running, made a risky decision. Believing that Kersee was the best track coach for her, she decided to follow him to UCLA, even though the school did not offer the courses she wanted.

Florence Griffith improved so quickly at UCLA that she was invited to the United States Olympic Trials in 1980. There she discovered the frustration of missing a dream by inches. Griffith came up just short of gaining a spot on the team in the 200-meter race. Adding to the frustration was the fact that it was her old rival, Valerie Brisco, who took that Olympic spot away from her.

The narrow defeat goaded Griffith on to greater efforts. In 1982 she finally claimed a bit of the spotlight for herself. That year she won the National Collegiate Athletic Association (NCAA) championship at 200 meters, with a time of 22.39 seconds.

Before this period, the sport of track and field had not been style-oriented. Most of the world's top performers were serious and intense when on the track, far more interested in results than in their appearance.

Florence wins the 200-meter event in the 1982 NCAA Championships while competing for UCLA. The next year she would win the 400-meter event.

Though dismaying track relay coaches, Florence's "talons" have endeared her to fashion manicurists.

Griffith was running vigorous workouts five days a week. Off the track, however, she was still flamboyant, dressing and looking different from most of her friends, just as she had since kindergarten. Florence wanted her creativity to be part of her success on the track. At UCLA she began to let her own style show by sporting long, brightly decorated fingernails.

"Fluorescent Flo" wins a spot on the 1984 Olympic Team.

Over the next two years, Florence worked hard to cut from her sprints those fractions of a second that had cost her an Olympic spot in 1980. At the 1984 Olympic Trials, she earned a position as a member of the United States team. She also earned the nickname "Fluorescent Flo" by first competing in shimmering bodysuits. Then, running before her hometown fans in the Games at Los Angeles, she sped to a second-place finish in the 200-meter dash. Her time of 22.04 just missed the old Olympic record for that event by one one-hundredth of a second. At first the feeling of the silver medal around her neck made her feel as though she had finally made her dream come true.

But soon the thrill of success mixed with other emotions. There on the victory stand beside her was the gold medal winner, Valerie Brisco. Brisco's three gold medals in the 1984 Olympics again pushed Griffith into the background. There was also the fact that the most powerful women's track teams in the world were not present at these Olympics. In 1980 the United States had boycotted the Olympics in Moscow. In response, the Soviet Union, East Germany, and their allies chose not to compete in 1984. There was serious doubt as to whether Griffith could have won even a bronze medal if the East Germans had raced. The recognition that Florence was striving for still remained beyond her reach.

Griffith's stubborn pride may also have cost her a

Florence doesn't appear quite satisfied despite winning a silver
medal in the 1984 Olympics. The other medalists are teammate
Valerie Brisco (gold) and Merlene Ottey of Jamaica (bronze).

gold medal in those Olympics. She had been contending for a spot on one of the United States' sprint-relay teams. But team officials looked at her dagger-like, six-inch-long fingernails and shook their heads. Such nails, they said, were too long to allow for a smooth baton pass during the relay. Griffith disagreed and refused to cut them. The relay teams ran, and won, without her.

This extreme mixture of joy and frustration left Griffith feeling drained. After the Olympics, she lost her enthusiasm for running. Although she did not quit altogether, she dropped out of hard training and gained 15 pounds. When she took a job in the employee relations department of a large company, it seemed her sprinting career might be over.

Al Joyner won the gold medal in the 1984 Olympic triple-jump event but failed to make the Olympic team in 1988. He has since switched events and hopes to make the 1992 squad as a hurdler.

4
Training to Win

Griffith discovered that it was not easy for her to escape the world of track and field. Even her new boyfriend was a constant reminder of the last Olympics. Al Joyner had won the gold medal in 1984 in his event, the triple jump.

Al had first seen Florence at the 1980 Olympic Trials. He then thought that she was the most "beautiful woman in the world." Although Florence was dating someone else, Al would occasionally meet her during the track seasons. Florence, however, paid little attention to him.

Early in 1986, Joyner left his Arkansas home to train in Los Angeles with his sister, Jackie. Jackie Joyner had long been a teammate of Florence's, first at UCLA and then at Bobby Kersee's World Class Athletic Club. In Los Angeles, Al pursued Florence with the same patience and determination that he had shown in his pursuit of the gold medal. Florence recalls that Al "devoted so much time to me, I was overwhelmed." Al's positive attitude was rewarded. The longer the couple stayed together, the more common interests they found they had, in life as well as track.

Not only was Al a world-class jumper, but so was his sister. By 1986 Jackie Joyner-Kersee was a favorite to win gold medals in the long jump and heptathlon in the next Olympics. She had also just married Bobby Kersee, who was both Florence's and her coach. With such influences, it is little wonder that Florence found herself drawn back into running in 1986.

But, by this time, she had found many other interests. In addition to working her regular job, Florence often hired herself out as a hairdresser. Some of the designs she created with hair-braiding took more than 12 hours to complete. She also became interested in writing stories when some of her 30 nephews and nieces repeatedly begged her for her bedtime tales. In what little time she had between these other activities, she headed for the spa or a park to do her workouts.

Her nephews and nieces, meanwhile, were doing their best to get her married. They encouraged Al so much that in the summer of 1987 he decided to ask Florence to be his wife. Al rented a limousine and proposed to her on his knees in the car. Florence said nothing that night. The next evening the couple was having dinner at a pizza parlor with two of Florence's nephews and nieces, Larry and Khalisha. Larry won

Jackie Joyner-Kersee is advised by Bobby Kersee, her husband and coach. These two, together with Al and Florence, would become known as the "first family" of track and field at the 1988 Olympics.

Florence signs autographs for some young fans.

a prize playing Skee-Ball and Khalisha grabbed it, saying, "This is perfect!" She gave it to Florence who slipped the prize, a yellow charm in the shape of the word "yes," to Al under the table.

28

In the next few months, Florence had a great deal to celebrate. At the World Championships in Rome, she placed second to East Germany's Silke Gladisch-Möller in the 200 meters. Then, long fingernails and all, she ran a strong third leg to help the United States' 4 x 100-meter relay team to first place. Finally, on October 10, 1987, Al and Florence were married.

In the next nine months, Florence Griffith Joyner developed from an excellent, but unspectacular, sprinter into an awesome power. The change took place quietly in two places: the training room and her mind. Her fine showing against top competition in Rome showed her that she was closer to the top than ever before. This spurred her on to work harder so that she could be the best. Florence sought out her old coach, Bobby Kersee, for some training guidance. With her husband, Al, as her workout partner and supervisor, Florence attacked the training program. When she was not running, she was building up her strength by lifting leg weights. Late at night, long after her main workout, she would finish her day with another run or more weight lifting.

Meanwhile, the change going on in her mind was even more important. While learning to work harder during training, she also learned not to work so hard on running. She discovered the reason why many fine athletes have suffered poor performances at important moments: They try too hard. The muscles of the body must work together smoothly in order to get the best results. Griffith Joyner discovered that she was pushing too hard, trying to force her muscles to go faster. This was making the muscles fight against each other. The key to running fast was not to strain every muscle to its limit but to relax and let them do their job.

Florence popularized the hooded uniform (opposite) at the 1987 World Championships in Rome, Italy, in addition to winning a gold and a silver medal. The hood would later be incorporated into the 1988 Olympic Team uniform.

5
Record-Breaking Races

As the athletes gathered in Indianapolis for the 1988 United States Olympic Trials, only a few people had a clue as to what was going to happen in the women's sprints. Most track and field magazines gave Griffith Joyner only brief mention. (Many did not know she was married and referred to her as "Florence Griffith.") They agreed that she had a good chance of making the Olympic team again in the 200 meters. Although she had posted the fastest United States times in 1985 and 1987 in the 100-meter race, she seemed more of a long shot to qualify at that distance. After all, she had seldom competed in that race, concentrating on the longer sprints instead. The most in-depth predictions of the Trials listed her among the six or seven runners who had a chance of placing behind world-record holder Evelyn Ashford.

But Bobby Kersee knew something the experts did

not. On a track at San Diego just a month before, he had timed Florence at 10.89 for 100 meters. Kersee knew that she had not run her best that day. On a better day, he thought, Florence could challenge Ashford's world record of 10.76.

Al Joyner was also in on the secret. Shortly before they had left Los Angeles, he had joined Dee Dee for a last late-night run. As usual, they began to race down a busy street to an intersection 700 meters away. Although he does not compete in sprints, Al Joyner could not have won the Olympic gold medal in the triple jump if he did not have blazing speed. That night he could stay with his wife for only the first 50 yards. When he reminded her to relax, she burst ahead of him as if she had discovered another gear. Al knew his wife was ready.

Florence Griffith Joyner, meanwhile, had another secret. She planned to stun her competitors with more than just her speed. Packed in her suitcase were 14 eye-catching outfits that were unlike anything that had been seen at an Olympic trials before. Many of them were of a radical design that had come to her by accident. She had been been experimenting with a new fashion design by cutting holes in some tights. While doing so she had cut one leg off completely. A quick glance in the mirror told her that she had stumbled upon an interesting look. With a mixture of her favorite brilliant colors and a few other ideas, she had prepared an athletic wardrobe that was certain to attract stares. As if that were not enough to set her apart from the field, there were the long fingernails. With a rainbow assortment of paints, she could create artwork to match any mood.

Florence knew very well that she was making herself the center of attention. She had briefly tried something like this the previous summer. At the World Championships in Rome, she had raced in a semifinal heat wearing a hooded bodysuit decorated with stars and stripes. But she had gone back to a more traditional suit for the finals. This time she was really going out on a limb. However, Florence's confidence was now as sharp as her image. With such thoughts in her mind, she was so anxious to run the Trials that she packed her bags two weeks ahead of time.

On July 16, Griffith Joyner settled into her starting blocks for the first qualifying heat of the 100-meter dash. A brisk wind was fanning the 11,000 fans who were sweltering in the 98°F (37°C) heat. At the sound of the gunshot, a green blur burst from the starting line. Dressed in her one-legged green suit, Florence easily pulled away from the pack and crossed the finish line all alone. The official time was 10.60, well under the world record!

It was an astounding opening race for someone who had never run the event in international competition. Yet the track world seemed more amused

Mental preparedness and concentration were keys to Florence's successes in the 1988 Olympic Trials. Notice her shirt, which reads, "Trying 4 the gold in '88."

by her outfit than amazed by her time. She had run well, but the time could not be taken seriously. In international competition races are run regardless of the wind speed. World records, however, do not count unless the tailing wind is 2 meters/sec (4.47 mph) or less. Everyone knew that Griffith Joyner must have been blown down the track by the wind. The wind gauge on the track had broken, so officials had been forced to examine a computer printout of wind readings. No one was surprised to find that the tailing wind had been almost twice the allowable.

Kersee and Griffith Joyner, though, sensed that the wind had not made as much difference as others thought. As they discussed her next race, they decided that conditions were ripe for a world record. The hot weather favored sprinters by keeping their muscles loose and limber. The Indianapolis track is considered one of the fastest, springiest tracks in the world. The noisy crowd would encourage the runners to give that extra effort.

Kersee advised Florence to test the wind while in the starting blocks for her next race. If it seemed to have calmed, she should go all out for the world record. If it was still strong, she should ease off slightly and save herself for another heat.

Two and a half hours after her first race, Florence Griffith Joyner kneeled in the starting blocks testing the wind. For this second heat she had chosen a shocking purple and turquoise one-legged suit and had painted her fingernails orange with white and black stripes on the tips. But there were so many things going on in her mind that she had no time to notice the stares. The wind was blowing steadily with occasional powerful gusts. On the infield of the track she could see her husband struggling in the triple jump. The competition there was fierce and Al was also having problems coping with the unpredictable wind.

As the sprinters were called to a set position, Griffith Joyner thought she detected a lull in the wind. The starting gun sounded and she broke from the starting line as if shot out of a sling. Down the track she blazed, her feet barely touching the 115°F (46°C) track. By the time she reached 50 meters, she was so far ahead she could have coasted to a win. But she kept concentrating on her strides, making sure that she reached out with each leg and that she did not start galloping. She checked to see that her arms and body were relaxed and in the proper position. Lifting her knees high at the end, she drove for the finish line.

The official time was 10.49, an incredible .27 seconds better than the world record! Ever since electronic timing had been introduced 20 years earlier, the women's 100-meter record had never been broken by more than .13 seconds. Again the spectators shook

Indisputable victory at last!

their heads and remarked about how the wind must have blown her down the track.

But when officials checked the wind gauge, they were dumbfounded to see it read 0.0! As news of this spread, the stadium buzzed with disbelief. Those in the stands had felt the wind during the race. The stadium flags had been practically snapping in the breeze. A wind gauge placed by the long jump pit, 15 meters from the track straightaway, had measured 2.9 meters per second, well over the allowable tailwind. At other times during the evening, world records by Willie Banks in the triple jump and Carl Lewis in the men's 100 meters had been disallowed because of wind. Did anyone really believe that, so late in her career, Florence Griffith Joyner could suddenly smash a world record to bits? Her own coach admitted being shocked that she could run 100 meters in only 10.49!

The makers of the Swiss Oneida wind-speed meter checked the wind gauge after the race and found it to be working perfectly. After a long discussion, they declared that the confusion had been caused by swirling winds. While the wind may have been blowing hard in one direction only a few feet away, it had been blowing in a different direction across the track straightaway. Griffith Joyner had run with the wind blowing across the track. It had not helped her, and therefore her world record would stand.

There were plenty who doubted that explanation, though. All of the times in the women's 100 meters had been fast. At the 1984 Olympic Trials, Evelyn Ashford had won the event with a time of 11.18.

Knowing that a quick, stable start is a requirement for winning results, Florence takes time to position herself in the starting blocks before each race.

This year that time would not have advanced her past the first round! Given the wind and the fast track, Griffith Joyner would have to prove again that she really was the fastest woman who had ever lived.

The skeptics did not have long to wait. The very next day, July 17, Florence reported for her semifinal heat dressed in an all-black, two-legged outfit. This time the wind had clearly subsided. But the results were the same. Again, Griffith Joyner rocketed down the track far ahead of her nearest rival. She crossed the finish line in 10.70. Although it was her slowest time of the competition, it was still faster than any other woman had ever run before.

That set up the final proof two hours later. Running head-to-head against Ashford in the finals, she would be testing her nerves as well as her legs. Wind or no wind, she would have a chance to measure herself against the former world-record holder. Her confidence seemingly boosted by her exotic fashion, Florence showed up for the crucial match in another head-turning outfit. This time it was a fluorescent blue and white suit, which she accented by painting her nails pink. Ashford and Griffith Joyner were placed side by side on the track. In the hush that preceded the start, nearly every pair of eyes was turned toward these two favored runners.

Florence bolted out of the blocks and began to surge ahead. Her relaxed strides began to put inches,

Florence waves the flag after easily winning the 100-meter final. Runner-up Evelyn Ashford (left) and the third-place finisher Gwen Torrence (middle) also qualify for the Olympic Team.

then feet between her and her rival. Halfway down the track, it was obvious that Griffith Joyner's times of the previous day were not wind-blown flukes.

Florence overtakes her long-time rival Valerie Brisco along the curve and goes on to set a new United States record in the 200 meters.

She breezed across the finish line in 10.61. The tail wind had been under the limit. Evelyn Ashford finished in 10.81, very close to her world-record time. Yet she had been beaten by four yards (3.6m), a wide margin in so short a race. Gwen Torrence had run a fine race, 10.91, yet had been left well behind in third place.

But Florence's colorful, inspired performance was only half over. In the first round of the 200-meter event, Florence took her first shot at Valerie Brisco's four-year-old United States record of 21.81. Even though she ran the curve poorly and pushed herself too hard, Griffith Joyner came close to the mark with a 21.96.

The luck of the draw put her in the same heat as Brisco in the semifinals. Wouldn't it be fitting, she thought, to break her long-time rival's record in head-to-head competition? This time when the gun sounded she stayed under control. She ran easily and smoothly around the curve until she hit the straightaway. Then her yellow shoes seemed electrically charged as she exploded into high gear. By the time she reached the finish line, there was an enormous gap between her and the second-place Brisco. Griffith Joyner's time of 21.77 was a new United States record.

Just when fans were wondering what more to expect from this new star, she appeared on the track for the final in an all-white lace body suit with matching white shoes. Even Florence had thought the outfit was too unusual to wear in competition. But on a dare from fellow sprinter Caryl Smith, she donned it at the last minute. By this time Florence had so dominated the sprints that her daring outfit seemed a natural compliment to her skill. Perhaps no one had ever run an Olympic trials in an "athletic negligée," but then neither had any woman ever run with such grace and speed. After many years of work and frustration, Griffith Joyner was making history and there was no doubt that she was doing it her way. No one was surprised to see her accelerate down the straightaway for an easy win in 21.85.

Until Griffith Joyner had burst onto the scene in Indianapolis, United States coaches had been edgy about their chances in the women's sprints in the Olympics. Missed in 1984, the East Germans would be on hand in Seoul, South Korea. Among their sprinters was long-legged Heike Drechsler, co-holder of the world record at 200 meters, and Silke Gladisch-Möller, who had won both the 100 and 200 at the 1987 World Championships in Rome. Many had expected the East Germans to defeat Ashford in the shorter race while holding on to their mastery of the 200, a race they had practically owned for many years. Suddenly, Griffith Joyner seemed to have the 100 locked up, with a good chance at taking the 200 as well.

Florence in her "athletic negligée."

The flame of the 24th Olympiad in Seoul, South Korea

6
Setting a New Pace

The Olympics would be different from the Trials. In Indianapolis Florence had surprised everyone. Now she would have to face the pressure of being the favorite. The splash she had made with her stunning track suits guaranteed that reporters would be hounding her wherever she went. She was no longer "Florence" or even "Dee Dee." "Flo Jo" was her new name among the media that swarmed around her.

Strong-willed as ever, Griffith Joyner began her final quest for gold by replacing her coach, Bobby Kersee. Her husband Al, who had failed in his attempt to make the USA team in the triple jump, would be her full-time coach. With an eye toward the 5' 11" Drechsler, Al ran alongside Flo Jo on striding drills. He wanted to make sure his 5' 7" wife was not thrown by the sight of Drechsler's long strides when the two ran side by side.

Florence arrived in Seoul, South Korea, knowing

that most of the work was behind her. All she had to do now was stay healthy and relax. She had not been in South Korea 10 minutes, however, before she discovered that there is no sure thing. While they were still in the airport, Al's baggage cart tipped over, landing on Florence's ankle! According to Florence, "It felt like a refrigerator fell on me."

So much for relaxation. All she could do was stay off her feet and hope that the injury responded to treatment. For several days she did nothing but stretch, put ice on her bruised Achilles tendon, and pray. Fortunately, the injury was less serious than it could have been. By the time her name was called for the first heat of the 100 meters, Flo Jo was ready to go. Earlier, she had written down two numbers in her diary: heat—10.62, final—10.54.

Olympic rules are more rigid than those of the Trials. In order to compete for the United States, Flo Jo had to wear an official team uniform, not one of her one-legged creations. Her taste for the unusual was satisfied by a hooded running suit that was part of the USA track team's wardrobe. Wearing the hood, she hit her goal right down to the hundredth of a second in the quarterfinals. Her 10.62 easily beat Ashford's old Olympic record of 10.97.

Griffith Joyner discarded the hood for her semifinal race. This would be an important test because Heike Drechsler had also been assigned to her heat.

Florence adjusts the hood of the newly designed Olympic suit.

Formidable East Germans Heike Drechsler (left) and Silke
Gladisch-Möller were Florence's chief competition in the 1988
Olympics.

Determined to put down the East German challenge at the first opportunity, Flo Jo primed herself to break out of the starting blocks the instant the starting gun sounded. Just as she exploded into action, though, the starter called the sprinters back. Flo Jo had jumped the gun by a fraction of a second.

Suddenly her gold medal quest was back in danger. Sprinters are allowed only one false start. If she so much as flinched while in her set position in the blocks, she would be disqualified.

Playing it safe, Flo Jo eased up in the starting blocks. As a result she got off to a slow start. But it did not matter. By 50 meters she had caught Drechsler and began pulling away from her. With her thick hair flowing behind her and a radiant smile spreading across her lips, she crossed the finish line all alone. The experts knew it was all over. Drechsler had run the best race of her life. Flo Jo had not and yet had easily bested her rival, 10.70 to 10.91.

By this time, Griffith Joyner's confidence had become unquenchable. Former Olympic sprint champion Wilma Rudolph remarked that Griffith Joyner walked onto the track for the finals as if she owned it. Two decades of running were about to pay off. Nothing could stop her.

As usual, she chatted briefly with her rivals. She even took time to assure a jittery Grace Jackson from Jamaica not to worry, that she would do just fine.

Then Flo Jo settled into her blocks. She placed her fingers, the nails decorated in colorful Olympic and United States symbols, behind the starting line.

The instant the gun sounded, Evelyn Ashford and Heike Drechsler churned furiously toward the finish line 100 meters away. But it was over almost from the start. Flo Jo pounced out of her blocks and grabbed the lead at once. Relaxed and flowing, she steadily stretched her lead. Sensing what she was doing, Griffith Joyner "felt so happy inside I just had to let it out." As her lead widened, so did her smile. Five meters from the finish she raised her arms in pure joy. Her gold medal time was a wind-aided 10.54, exactly what she had set as her goal! Ashford, who edged Drechsler for second place, 10.83 to 10.85, just shook her head in disbelief.

In the 200 meters, Flo Jo continued to dominate the sprints. Shortly after watching her sister-in-law, Jackie Joyner-Kersee, win the gold medal in the long jump, Griffith Joyner breezed into the record books with a 21.56 in a qualifying heat. In the process she looked as relaxed as if she was chasing jackrabbits on a lonely desert trail. Her race in the finals was a thing of beauty from start to finish. Flo Jo glided easily around the curve, grabbed the lead, and surged effortlessly into a higher gear. Lighting the track with her trademark smile, she crossed the finish line in an incredible 21.34, the new world record.

Maintaining her perfect stride, Florence pulls away from Heike Drechsler (left), Russian Natalya Pomoshnikova (middle), and Jamaican Grace Jackson (far right) to win the 100-meter race and her first gold medal.

Despite her camera-pleasing style, Flo Jo showed that she was willing to sacrifice personal glory for the good of the team. In the 4 x 100 relay, the team's best sprinter is usually allowed to run the finishing leg.

Flo Jo, however, gracefully returned to the number three position she had run in Rome. She did not, however, yield on the matter of her fingernails. This time, the coaches gave in to her wishes. Despite Flo Jo's sloppy handoff, she kept the United States team just close enough for Ashford to come from behind in the anchor leg to win the gold medal.

Perhaps Griffith Joyner's most courageous effort came in her only moment of disappointment. Striving for a fourth gold medal, she accepted the challenge of running the final leg of the women's 4 x 400-meter relay. Taking the baton from Valerie Brisco, she started her leg just behind the Soviets and she remained within striking distance to the very end. It took a world-record effort by the Soviets to edge her out and deprive her of that fourth victory.

Florence Griffith Joyner left Seoul, South Korea, with three gold medals and one silver. She owned the seven fastest times ever run in the women's 100 meters. Flo Jo had smashed the previous records for 100 and 200 meters as they had never been smashed before. She had done it, not with joyless, machine-like precision, but with a sparkle and a free-flowing grace all her own.

Because of her dominance of the women's sprinting events Florence garnered five prestigious awards. She won the C. C. Jackson Award for outstanding woman track athlete of 1988 and she was named Associated

Press Female Athlete of the Year. Her performance was recognized internationally by the Soviet news agency, Tass, when it named her Athlete of the Year.

Florence's third gold medal came in the 4 x 100-meter relay. The members of the team are (left to right) Alice Brown, Sheila Echols, Flo Jo, and Evelyn Ashford.

Florence also won the 1988 Sullivan Award, which is given to the top amateur athlete in the United States, and the Jesse Owens Award for the outstanding track and field athlete of the year.

In explaining why she had taken up running, Florence Griffith Joyner put it simply. "Sprinting is excitement!" she said. Never has that been more true than when Flo Jo breezed through the summer of 1988.

FLORENCE GRIFFITH JOYNER'S RACING ACHIEVEMENTS

YEAR	MEET	EVENT	TIME	RESULT
1982	NCAA Championships	200m	22.39	Collegiate Champion
1983	NCAA Championships	400m	50.94	Collegiate Champion
1984	Olympics	200m	22.04	Silver Medal
1987	World Championships	200m	21.96	Silver Medal
1987	World Championships	4x100m relay	41.58 (team)	Gold Medal
1988	Olympic Trials	100m	10.49	World Record
1988	Olympic Trials	200m	21.77	U.S. Record
*1988	Olympics	100m	10.54 (wind-aided)	Gold Medal
1988	Olympics	200m	21.34	World Record and Gold Medal
1988	Olympics	4x100m relay	41.98 (team)	Gold Medal
1988	Olympics	4x400m relay	3:15.51 (team)	Silver Medal

*Olympic Record 10.62 in quarterfinal

ACKNOWLEDGEMENTS

The photographs are reproduced through the courtesy of: Paul J. Sutton, pp. 1, 2, 6, 8, 20, 24, 32, 36, 41, 43, 51, 52; Robert Tringali Jr., pp. 10, 39, 55, 57, 59, 60; David Starr, Jordan High School, p. 15; Steven E. Sutton, pp. 18, 19, 27; David Madison, pp. 22, 28; Iundt/Ruszniewski, p. 31; Mitchell B. Reibel, pp. 44, 47; Korean Overseas Information Service, p. 48. Front cover: David Madison. Back cover: Steven E. Sutton.